LiME:
LEADERSHIP in MOTION & EXPERIENCE

A Proven Model for Unleashing Greatness

Ephraim Osaghae MBA, MBL

All rights reserved.

No one is permitted to reproduce or transmit any part of this book through any means or form, be it electronic or mechanical. No one also has the right to store the information herein in a retrieval system, nor do they have the right to photocopy, record copies, scan parts of this document, etc., without the proper written permission of the publisher or author.

ISBN 978-0-6453744-7-6

Copyright © 2022
Ephraim Osaghae

TABLE OF CONTENTS

DEDICATION v
ACKNOWLEDGMENT vii
FOREWORDS ix

CHAPTER 1: INTRODUCTION 1
CHAPTER 2: LiME AND GREATNESS 7
CHAPTER 3: LEADERSHIP 17
CHAPTER 4: MOTION 27
CHAPTER 5: EXPERIENCE 37
CHAPTER 6: LiME TRIALS AND TRIUMPHS 51
CHAPTER 7: CONCLUSION 59

DEDICATION

To the maiden LiME participants:

King David Oyewopo, Keyshiaa Menezes, Harmoniche Deng, Maria Shyllon, Odaro Osaghae, Esther Batty, Solotin Santana, Gracia Ngandu, Abraham Oyewopo, Fatiha Enilari, Joshuaa Menezes, Joy Ngandu, David Okiwelu, Saskia Wilson, Victor Komaiya, Efe Osaghae, Osamu Frederick, Emeline Niyokwizigira, Marcus Wilson, Olivia Amudo, Jaden Samuel, Thabo Mazibuko, Chuks Anwasi, Sanchez Zowunu, and Samuel Chansongo.

You are the proven models for unleashing greatness.

ACKNOWLEDGMENT

Recognising the Great Minds that Teamed Up to Implement the LiME Vision

The LiME initiative would not have been as successful without the support of the parents' group. The parents' connection to the vision was an early win and a critical success factor. The financial commitment, the venue drop-offs, and the pick-ups after that were priceless. Some of the parents even became part of volunteers for LiME. They also formed part of the LiME Parent Group WhatsApp page, where they kept the ongoing connection, communication, encouragement, and support. They are Neil & Lea Menezes, Louis & Omoye Okiwelu, Nestor & Agness Ngandu, Martin & Yuni Liem, Ebun Enilari, Martin & Amy Deng, Marlon & Bonny Wilson, Ephraim

& Esosa Osaghae, Femi & Oludotun Oyewopo, Lakers & Morenikeji Komaiya, Frederick & Joy Idehen, Emmanuel & Victoria Shyllon, Marco Issaya & Leocadia Niyonkuru, Sipho & Thobile Mazibuko, James & Beena Samuel, Fred & Mukuka Chansongo, Richard & Elizabeth Amudo, Lawrence & Nwakego Anwasi, and Mary Zowonu.

LiME coordinators, facilitators, mentors and special guests and their significant contributions deserve acknowledgement. They include Ephraim Osaghae, Femi Oyewopo, Samuel Shyllon, Richard Amudo, John & Brenda Palmer, Emma Kake, Liam Palmer, Lakers Komaiya, Rohit & Lakshmi Kanchi, Gabriel Adesanya, Esther Mwathi, Cornelius Itotoh, Natasha Van Wyk, Mireille Toulekima, Caroline Surtees, Kim Charles, Gladys Serugga (Miss Africa Perth 2018), Glenn Dewhurst (Mayor of City of Gosnells 2017 – 2019), Paul Ng (Mayor of City of Canning 2015 – 2019), and Hon Bill Johnston. They went beyond the usual call for support to ensure the smooth running of the LiME initiative.

Finally, a big shout out to LiME Sponsors to date (cash and kind): City of Gosnells, City of Canning, Perth Airport, Department of Communities, Relationship Australia WA, BHP, Afropacific Media, and Business Station.

FOREWORDS

LiME Academy is more than a club to me. It has become a second family. When I was first introduced to this fantastic community in 2018, there was no hesitation in accepting me with open arms and starting me on my journey of unleashing greatness. Without knowing it, I began to uncover hidden potentials and implement new strategies to lead a better life.

So far, words cannot describe how much LiME has impacted me. I've cultivated my leadership, communication, and a wide variety of life-essential skills, which in turn has brought me many opportunities, including both local and international recognition, and has shaped me into a dynamic youth who is prepared for the adult world.

- Harmoniche "Niche" Deng, LiME Participant / Co-Author of 'A Handbook for Migrant Youth'

LiME Academy has been a unique and positive experience for me. Through LiME Academy, I have learned how to be a leader, do excellent public speaking, use Artificial Intelligence, and much more. Ephraim has been a great inspiration throughout the experience, always providing helpful, valuable feedback and building my confidence.

LiME Academy has helped me to achieve my dream of becoming an author and taught me that failing isn't the end. I now always 'Fail Fast', 'Fail Small', and 'Fail Forward'. Through this book, I hope you can gain confidence in many aspects of your lives as an audience.

- Keyshiaa Menezes, LiME Participant / Co-Author of 'A Handbook for Migrant Youth'

My time spent at LiME was productive and enjoyable. I found the initiative to be quite engaging. The ideas and information provided have undoubtedly found their way into my daily life and routines. It was an excellent introduction to becoming a leader in my environment.

I picked up a few essential pieces of knowledge that have significantly boosted my capacity to lead others and, perhaps more crucially, myself. Because of the initiative's infectious enthusiasm and boundless prospect for growth,

I've adopted a winning attitude in the face of my biggest challenges. In addition, I've had the opportunity to form meaningful connections with my peers, which I will always cherish.

- King David Oyewopo, LiME Participant / Co-Author of 'A Handbook for Migrant Youth'

I have been part of the LiME journey from its beginning as a mentor and leader. I have witnessed how the program has helped youth grow as leaders, be self-aware of their unique gifts, step into greatness and become the best version of themselves. It was also an excellent opportunity to learn from the other mentors and leaders who dedicated their time to the growth of our leaders of tomorrow. I think the LiME program is a key enabler in creating a bridge between formal and informal education. I highly recommend it. It is a transformative platform of excellence for the youth.

- Mireille Toulekima, Award-Winning Global Entrepreneur / Engineer / Thought Leader / STEM & Energy Expert / TOP 100 Female executive in the oil and gas industry in Africa / G100 Global Chair Engineering. A LiME Mentor.

Our son continually appreciates his identity. LiME has provided him with a platform to learn life's essential skills of leadership, healthy relationships, finance, and technology, which are the needed ingredients for today's innovative era. As parents, we believe that the LiME project could be a catalyst to a promising future for youth and prepare them for the ever-changing world.

- Joy & Fred Idehen, Health professionals and Parents of a LiME Participant

CHAPTER 1
INTRODUCTION

In the last quarter of 2017, sharing a strategic space with some stakeholders, it became clearer that I was carrying a burden. I saw the pivotal role I needed to play in catalysing several success stories and greatness. This urge birthed a passion for using my leadership skills, voice, and network of reliable collaborators to blaze the transformation trail through a youth empowerment initiative called LiME, Leadership in Motion and Experience.

Here's a Bit of My Story:

"As part of my upbringing and teenage years, I was exposed to the model of life that takes the focus beyond just self, to caring for the need of others around me as well. It is freeing to avoid the extra burden of "performing" and putting up an impression for the approval of others, including peers. Exposure to suitable models and leaders caused a shift in the right direction for me. I asked questions as much as necessary. I was open to feedback and guidance. I intentionally followed through with actions that ensured continuous improvement and growth. It hasn't been a perfect run to date. However, I have learned I'm human; errors and failures were mostly learning points for growth and leadership."

LiME founder, Ephraim Osaghae

INTRODUCTION

Down the road of my journey in diaspora, I have encountered a remarkable dynamism in youth and other stakeholders. Sadly, I've also found many young minds, including those from culturally diverse backgrounds, struggling to express their greatness despite their potential and abilities. However, due to the LiME initiative, many young people (mostly 12 – 17 years of age) have been trained, mentored, and inspired in multiple aspects of life, leadership, and other transformative future-ready skills.

The outcome has gladdened my heart because these *LiMErs* have proven a model that can be replicated and scaled for more success. This book aims to share the LiME story from my viewpoint as the founder, leader, and key custodian of the vision to date. Reaching out to youth and younger people is the main trigger, hence using the LiME youth initiative as a case study and model. However, the lessons can inspire and motivate a broader audience of individuals and groups to recognise their potential in harnessing and securing the future they deserve.

Readers and users of this book will learn about the importance of leadership, motion (being active and agile), and experience in the context of achieving greatness. It would highlight relevant aspects of LiME and its core activities that have continued to inspire the proper intentionality, envisioning, mindfulness, self-discovery, self-worth, and valuable networks in leadership. It presents snapshots of how participants addressed common life issues relating to identity, conflicting priorities, peer influence, self-esteem, and motivation while channelling their energy towards experiential successes in personal, social, economic, educational, and leadership development.

This book does not render expert advice on the issues discussed. Instead, it offers insights into fundamental leadership principles, experiential knowledge, and proven approaches to managing life, leading impact, and achieving success.

INTRODUCTION

I have provided stories and documentaries based on my experience as the founder, convener, parent, concerned global citizen, coach, and project leader at this remarkable LiME initiative. If this book contributes to bringing you to the same place of purposeful and intentional investment in self and youth, thereby redeeming the future for many generations, then this effort yielded the desired result. As this book transforms and inspires young and learning minds to do life better, I've succeeded.

It's time to unleash greatness!

CHAPTER 2
LiME AND GREATNESS

"I am not afraid of an army of lions led by a sheep; I am afraid of an army of sheep led by a lion."

- Alexander The Great

Why explore the topic of "greatness"? A wise man once said it's not the good or negative power that dominates a system; it's the greater power! The weak are dominated by the strong; the small, by the great—this is true for every life form. Life works this way. It's the responsibility of individual players to seek greater heights and live sustainably in their greatness.

Some people may be able to attain the heights by themselves, hardly though. Others, more likely, would require some form of guidance, peer support, and leadership to get there and, hopefully, keep growing from there. The LiME core involves teaching, challenging, and inspiring youth of diverse cultural backgrounds to discover themselves and their potential in unleashing their greatness.

LiME Participants and Their BHP Excursion[1]

---

[1] A Handbook for Migrant Youth: Peer To Peer Wisdom From Those Who've Been There, Done That (2019: 8).

LiME Participants and Their BHP Excursion [2]

Participating in the Process of Greatness[3]

---

[2] *A Handbook for Migrant Youth: Peer To Peer Wisdom From Those Who've Been There, Done That (2019: 8).*
[3] Ibid, (2019: 32)

So, What Exactly is Greatness?

"A Man's greatness lies in his power of thoughts."
- Blaise Pascal

Greatness is generally considered a state of consciousness of being better than others in a particular place or context. While some people attribute greatness to individuals who possess a natural ability to be better than others, we focus on achieving excellence through learning and practice.

LiME inspires participants to aim and engage in being the best version of themselves rather than competing against others. Nevertheless, it starts right from the state of mind. One must begin from within enroute to attain true greatness. The pattern, the firmness, and the power of our thoughts largely determine our level of greatness. Anybody can achieve greatness if they hunger for it and dare to pursue growth and excellence along the way.

The LiME Perspective

LiME focused on three pillars of greatness - leadership, motion, and experience. They also constituted the delivery pathways for the initiative. Discovering self is a core foundation for greatness. It is more of an inside work from the LiME perspective. You can only develop, improve, and establish yourself when you know yourself. Thereafter, or at least simultaneously, one can begin to work outward, including acquiring relevant skills, growing in maturity, leading others, maintaining agility and dynamism for sustainable growth, and sharing experiences for more significant impact.

Leadership for Greatness

"The price of greatness is responsibility."
- Winston Churchill

LiME places significant emphasis on mastering the leading of self, working from the inside to the outside. It is about taking responsibility for oneself and pursuing the success one deserves. The core parts of the leadership training sessions involved self-discovery, self-awareness, self-discipline, etc., leading into segments on traditional leadership skills. LiMErs learned the full spread of practical aspects of personality types, self-worth, breaking the self-entitlement cycle, healthy mindset for leadership and envisioning. They acquired skills in goal-setting, motivation, resilience, time management, discipline, communication, etc.

Motion for Greatness

"Agility is a factor in greatness."
- Ephraim Osaghae

Everything is in motion; there is hardly anything static in life. Stagnation is a sign of failure to develop or advance further. Motion for greatness in the context of LiME means the dynamism, agility, or change required to thrive in our contemporary world. It is another factor that contributes to greatness indeed. LiME participants interactively exposed themselves to new technologies. Artificial Intelligence and robotics were part of the LiME program, including hands-on experience and learning how these technologies change the landscape of work, play, and our future. The immediate impact was evident when LiME organisers received positive feedback that the participants engaged their parents, guardians, and teachers on wise changes to career choices. Relevant and safe physical exercises (including outdoor activities like camping) were also regular features of LiME. These activities contributed significantly to their overall agility and boosted their mental health for greatness.

Experience for Greatness

"Nothing ever becomes real till it is experienced."
                                                    - John Keats

Experience, whether good or bad, has a way of shaping one's mind. They give you a better and clearer vision of what you didn't understand before, opening your eyes to a new challenge. Overall, it makes life endeavours real for you so that you get better at them.

One will face challenges on the path to greatness. Failure may seem like a setback, but in the true sense, it's a stepping stone. When you fail and want to start again, you know the errors you made in the first attempt. Therefore, you will be safeguarded not to make them again. Consequently, a key takeaway for LiME participants is the saying: "fail fast, fail small, and fail forward.", LiME presenters (Lakers Komaiya and Femi Oyewopo), deserve the credit for adopting this poignant phrase during LiME leaving a positive mark on the minds of LiMErs. They still talk about the significant learning experience to date.

Greatness comes with expanded knowledge and an increasing network of positive influence. We might fail when we put ourselves out there and be vulnerable to learning opportunities. But we fail fast this way. Why delay the "failure" or learning experience? We also ensure that it's a minor failure, not one that will completely derail our vision. We must learn from every 'failure' to ensure that the experience moves us forward. Overall, the gains significantly exceed the pains.

The experiential aspect of LiME has been implemented via four components to date. Firstly, our mentorship brings selective mentors from diverse industry base to engage, inspire, and fill in the gaps for LiMErs. The sessions were planned and executed with the required intentionality to ensure that LiME participants had enough access to the relevant mentors per their aspirations.

The second component is our highly successful industry excursions. For example, we had a memorable day trip to BHP's Integrated Remote Operations Centre (IROC). BHP staff on the day explained and demonstrated to LiMErs, in real-time, the innovative capability of the centre to give an overview of their entire Western Australian mining network at a glance. The LiME team was also treated to a lunch / Q&A session where LiMErs interacted with some of the brightest BHP professionals and staff. What an unforgettable experience!

Thirdly, the experience of LiMErs engaging in a project together as a team was another remarkable achievement. They brainstormed and selected to write a book about their experience as a culturally diverse group in Australia. They then brainstormed further to agree on a topic, researched it (along with the subtopics), and wrote on it. Mentors supported them along the way, and Ephraim Osaghae collated their writings. That birthed their book:

A Handbook for Migrant Youth: Peer To Peer Wisdom From Those Who've Been There, Done That - published 13 August 2019.

Finally, LiMErs undertook another leadership-by-doing project where they led a 7-part live podcast series on relevant topics, including multiculturalism, education, employment, technology, social media, mental health, and finance. They engaged with the community, especially youth and younger people like them. They shared relevant knowledge, inspiration, and experiences. LiMErs are still receiving feedback on the positive and social impact of the series.

In a world with a deficit of great leaders, we must continue to support and promote proven models like LiME that will help identify, mobilise, articulate, harness, scale, and disperse the leadership skills of young people and others with open minds and learning hearts to engage. It creates a better world.

CHAPTER 3
LEADERSHIP

"If your actions inspire others to dream more, learn more, do more, and become more, you are a leader."

John Quincy Adams

What is Leadership?

Leadership means many things to many people, especially in our current world. Naturally, we begin our understanding of any concept from the place of promises and personal benefits. Hence, the first question is not about leadership but why I should care. Why do we need another book on leadership?

LiME: LEADERSHIP in MOTION & EXPERIENCE

LiME Participants and Leaders [4]

---

[4] A Handbook for Migrant Youth: Peer To Peer Wisdom From Those Who've Been There, Done That (2019: 2, 3, 4, 11, 12, 32, 66).

Leadership has been defined, debated, discussed, and demystified, yet it's still demanded, disgraced, and disfigured in our world today. There are social icons, classroom intellectuals, business owners, glamorous models, and digital space influencers who pride themselves in their number of followers and the significant, spell-binding influence they exert.

Leadership holds destinies — yours, mine, and everyone in the sphere of influence. It can equip us for success. It can enable us to become the best version of ourselves. It can amplify our impact in helping others to unlock their full potential. Leadership is critical to young people and other stakeholders in self-actualisation, nation-building, and sustainable futures.

Learning from Legends

There are diverse aspects of leadership, like experts in the field, including leadership styles, leadership processes, people management, performance management, conflict resolution, etc. A naïve perspective would focus on leadership as a position or status, but it has a broader scope. Based on the content and context of this book, let's consider some insights from three leaders who have been undeniably legendary in their global impact: John Maxwell[5], Oprah Winfrey[6], and Barack Obama[7].

John Maxwell is a No. 1 New York Times bestselling author, coach, and speaker. According to Maxwell:

"True leadership is about becoming better in all areas of life and inspiring others in your sphere to do the same."

He described leadership as *"influence – nothing more, nothing less."* Thus, it's how one can inspire others to do what is right.

Oprah Winfrey is an American talk show host, television producer, actress, author, and philanthropist. Sometimes called the "Queen of All Media", she was the richest African-American of the 20th century, once the world's only black billionaire, and one of the most outstanding black philanthropists in history. Arguably, she has been the most influential woman in the world. In her words:

> *"Leadership is about empathy. It is about being able to relate to and connect with people to inspire and empower their lives."*

---

[5] https://www.johnmaxwell.com/
[6] https://www.oprah.com/
[7] https://www.barackobama.com/

Barack Obama was the first African-American President of the United States and served two terms from 2009 to 2017. He was named the 2009 Nobel Peace Prize laureate. An excerpt of his official farewell address in 2017 indicates his leadership style and global influence:

> *"It has been the honour of my life to serve you. I won't stop. In fact, I will be right there with you, as a citizen, for all my remaining days. But for now, whether you are young or whether you're young at heart, I do have one final ask of you as your President — the same thing I asked when you took a chance on me eight years ago. I'm asking you to believe. Not in my ability to bring about change — but in yours. I am asking you to hold fast to that faith written into our founding documents; that idea whispered by slaves and abolitionists; that spirit sung by immigrants and homesteaders and those who marched for justice; that creed reaffirmed by those who planted flags from foreign battlefields to the surface of the moon; a creed at the core of every American whose story is not yet written: Yes, we can. Yes, we did. Yes, we can. Thank you. God bless you."*

The points by Maxwell, Winfrey, and Obama reignite the age-old question: are leaders born or made? Were these three outstanding leaders born or made?

John Maxwell provided a glimpse on his webpage into his background captioned *Small town, huge dreams*[8]. He attributed his success mainly to his unstoppable desire to make a difference in people's lives. Starting his career as a pastor in a small church, he embarked on developing himself and connecting with others. In his words: *"I've stayed a student of personal growth and development. Why? Because I believe it has the power to change us individually, connect communities, be a catalyst to corporations, and transform countries worldwide."* He subscribes to life-long learning.

Oprah Winfrey has been very open in relaying that she didn't become an overnight success but instead had a rough start in life[9]. Nevertheless, she worked her way up the ladder to become arguably one of the highest points on earth. She was born into poverty to a single teenage mother; she was molested during her childhood and early teenage years and became pregnant at fourteen; she had a son that was born prematurely and died in infancy. She

---

[8] https://www.johnmaxwell.com/my-purpose/
[9] https://en.wikipedia.org/wiki/Oprah_Winfrey

was sent to live with the man she calls her father, Vernon Winfrey, a barber in Nashville, Tennessee. She landed a job in radio while still in high school and worked her way to the very top in the entertainment industry, including founding her network, the Oprah Winfrey Network (OWN). She has since been inducted into the National Women's Hall of Fame and won many accolades and awards, too numerous to list here. She has been widely praised for overcoming adversity to become a benefactor and leader to many others, including global followership. Let's conclude that Oprah worked for her leadership with this quote from her: *"The big secret in life is that there is no big secret. Whatever your goal, you can get there if you're willing to work."*

Barack Obama did not get to the top as quickly as some thought. He was born in Honolulu, Hawaii. He worked as a community organiser in Chicago after graduating from Columbia University in 1983. He was the first black President of the Harvard Law Review, Harvard Law School 1988. After graduating, he became a civil rights attorney and an academic, teaching constitutional law at the University of Chicago Law School from 1992 to 2004. Then, turning to elective politics, he represented the 13th district in the Illinois Senate from 1997 until 2004, when he ran for the U.S. Senate and won. In 2008, after a close primary campaign against Hillary Clinton, he was nominated by the Democratic Party for President. Obama was elected the first African-American President of the United States over Republican nominee John McCain in the general election. He was inaugurated alongside his running mate Joe Biden in 2009. He served two terms from 2009 to 2017. Again, a quote from Obama would provide a pointer that he worked on his leadership journey: *"Keep dreaming. Keep asking why. Don't settle for what you already know. Never stop believing in the power of your ideas, imagination, and hard work to change the world."*

The belief that ***leaders are made*** was a foundational aspect of LiME. In alignment with the legends, we built leadership that takes the focus away from being just about you (and feeling entitled) to positively influencing the world and people around you to dream more, do more, and become more because of you. Indeed, this can be learned, doable, and growable!

The LiME Perspective: Mastering the Inner Game and Leading Inside-Out

There are some notable correlations between some of the keywords from the legends and the foundational LiME pillars: *belief; change; connect; empathy; influence; service; inspiring; becoming better; yes, we can; yes, we did.*

LiME emphasises the need to master the leading of self and then others. It is about taking responsibility for oneself and pursuing the success one deserves while impacting others along the way.

Cultural intelligence was also a crucial part of mastering the inner game. With a diversity of participants from fourteen different national and cultural backgrounds, specific focus was placed on empathy, respect, learning to connect, and team spirit.

The leadership training sessions involved facilitator-led components on self-discovery, self-awareness, self-worth, self-belief, self-discipline, etc. The participants learned practical aspects of personality types, breaking the self-entitlement cycle, a healthy mindset for leadership, envisioning, motivation, resilience, etc. They also acquired traditional leadership skills like goal-setting, time management, progress and change management, communication, conflict resolution, etc. We implemented different delivery methods based on participants' learning styles, including classrooms, audiovisuals, modelling, role-playing, outdoor activities, etc.

Communication skills were also a key focus for LiME. We used the established and highly successful Gavel Club system of Toastmasters International. It involved public speaking and leadership development components where LiMErs embarked on projects in stages that measurably improved their communication skills. LiME has been supported by seasoned communicators, leaders, and distinguished Toastmasters from District 17 of Toastmasters International Australia, who provided real-time feedback and mentorship during LiME Gavel sessions.

The narratives of the following two chapters relate to motion and experience. They further highlight how LiME participants were trained and mentored to lead from the inside out.

CHAPTER 4
MOTION

"The illiterate of the 21st century will not be those who cannot read and write, but those who cannot learn, unlearn, and relearn."

– Alvin Toffler

Motion is the action of moving or being moved. It's a response to change in the context of this book. This chapter highlights the need for agility in quickly and wisely responding to the dynamics of one's environment. How we run, ride, and skip through the hurdles of life matters a lot.

Adaptive skills are increasingly crucial in sustainable leadership; this was an intentional part of the LiME design and delivery. Fun-based physical activities were also regular LiME features in recognition of the need to maintain the boost in mental well-being.

Change and Leadership in Motion

Change is inevitable. It happens even when we do nothing! Unprecedented changes are associated with life and everyday living, including education, technology, work, media, culture, etc. So when a person decides against using their energy to benefit self, family, and society and thinks things will be at a standstill, they will be ready to receive a shock. Things are constantly changing in life. The only difference will be that the person won't be in control, but rather, they will be moved around by change. Alternatively, they can be intentional in leading the change they desire.

Intentional leadership, as we taught, promoted, and did with LiME, involves engaging in actions and activities that are thoughtful and deliberate to get desired results or outcomes. It is the opposite of doing nothing and hoping things turn out right. Worse still, some persons assume the attitude of feeling entitled, as if the world owes them some form of success despite their inaction. LiMErs were taught, inspired, and mentored to be agile in their leadership development and pursuits. Such adaptive leadership anticipates change, engaging in the process, working with uncertainties, changing when and where necessary, and thriving and celebrating while on the journey to achieving goals. It is leadership in motion.

Envisioning has been a critical aspect of intentional leadership in LiME. Youth and young people often face distractions from themselves, their peers, the media, etc. Even in cases where they have visions, the latter could be clouded, diluted, or even cancelled out by these distractions and diversions. LiMErs are taught and mentored to value, reignite and reshape their visions, including the dynamism of forming new ones where applicable. Technology advancement and implications for the future of work and career choices were a key focus for the last couple of LIME sessions.

Technology Advancement and Need for Change

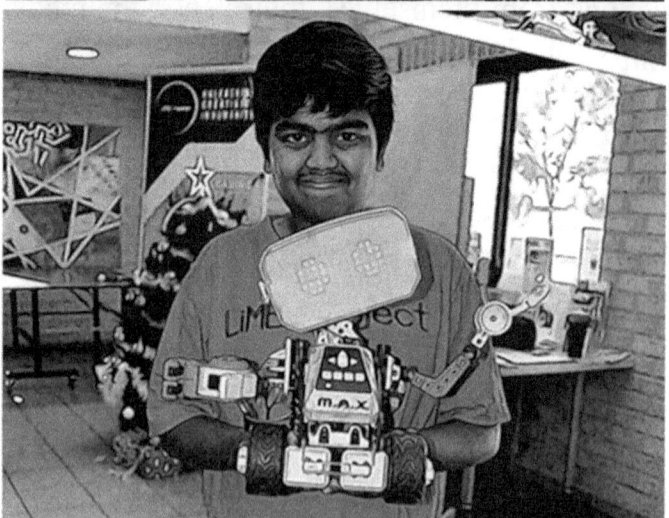

LiME Participants and Interaction with Technology[10]

---

[10] *A Handbook for Migrant Youth: Peer To Peer Wisdom From Those Who've Been There, Done That* (2019: 42, 49).

Artificial intelligence (AI) is now widely acknowledged as a disruptive technology that is changing the dynamics of the future of work. It is envisaged that the workplace will increasingly entail humans and machines working together, cooperatively, and harmoniously. In essence, AI can augment human decision-making, bringing more complex problem-solving and impartial data analysis to the boardroom than previously possible while valuing human creativity and innovation. Expectedly, AI will replace the more complex and routine elements of work. Managers need to lean toward more uniquely natural or human skills to succeed in the future. For example, motivating employees and enhancing creativity in the workplace cannot be downloadable; they're soft skills.

To this effect, LiME participants were actively and interactively exposed to new technologies. Part of the LiME program included Artificial Intelligence and robotics, where participants acquired hands-on experience and explicit knowledge of how these technologies are transforming the world. The technology series featured live AI and robotics sessions and how these developments are causing disruptions in how we work in the future. Rohit and Lakshmi Kanchi, now famously known as our

"AI couple," anchored that series for LiME with many takeaways and immediate applications.

They introduced LiMErs to "Max", a "cheeky" robot specifically built and programmed for LiME. It included live demonstrations where Max interacted with LiME participants, including holding intelligent conversations. It was an eye-opener and provided a sense of the disruptions ahead of us. Some LiMErs have taken it further as part of the school's special subject areas and electives. Feedback received over time has indicated that those sessions have caused a few changes in career aspirations now that they are more informed about the future and sustainability. LiMErs have learned to be more agile!

Leadership in Motion: Recreation, Physical Activities, and Fun

Recreation and fun activities are essential for boosting creativity. Recreation consists of activities or experiences carried on within leisure, usually chosen voluntarily by the participant—either because of satisfaction, pleasure, or creative enrichment derived or because he perceives specific personal or social values to be gained from them.

LiME was intentionally designed to involve regular recreational activities, indoors and outdoors, mainly in between training and mentoring sessions. However, it did provide real-time benefits for participants physically, mentally, and emotionally. The activities also contributed to enriching self-expression, interpersonal skills, friendship, and team building as they interacted with their peers over an event, game, etc.

LiME: LEADERSHIP in MOTION & EXPERIENCE

LiME and Fun Sessions[11]

---

[11] *A Handbook for Migrant Youth: Peer To Peer Wisdom From Those Who've Been There, Done That* (2019: 9).

MOTION

LiME and Fun Sessions[12]

---

[12] *A Handbook for Migrant Youth: Peer To Peer Wisdom From Those Who've Been There, Done That* (2019:74)

In addition to the site-based recreational activities, which were part of our regular LiME sessions, the youth were also taken to a camp away from the hustle and bustle of the city. Sessions of indoor and outdoor games were standard features with adequate safety provisions. Certified professionals assisted with managing the camping program, including full compliance with government regulations. Physical activities and personal development sessions focused on allowing the youth and young people in attendance to tap into and exercise their creativity to the maximum. Those sessions were fun! They contributed to building their adaptive and agile leadership skills. Overall, they demonstrated leadership in motion.

CHAPTER 5
EXPERIENCE

"Every experience is a positive experience if I view it as an opportunity for growth and self-mastery."

Brain Tracy

Global leaders and executives often use the 70-20-10 rule to learn, grow, and engage in change throughout their careers. According to this rule, one would need to have three types of experience to learn and grow as a leader in the following ratio:

- 70% experiences (including learning-by-doing, taking on new challenges, and going outside your comfort zone),

- 20% developmental relationships (learning from other people); and

- 10% coursework and training.

Indeed, experiential knowledge and learning are not restricted to academic and workplace environments. LiME was never meant to be another fancy trademark. Instead, it's a calling to leverage experience and insight for unleashing greatness in our youth. This chapter highlights the significance of the learning experience and critical insights from the LiME model.

Dynamics of Learning Through Experience and Reasoning

Experience is knowledge. The things we know from our experiences are said to be experiential knowledge. This knowledge becomes cemented as understanding is gained from seeing, feeling, and engaging in the things and events around us. It is based on actual lived experiences as opposed to theories and imaginations. Experiential learning is valuable in improving one's competency and skill levels. It often entails pushing you out of your comfort zone, stretching your skills, and challenging your abilities as part of the growth process.

Lessons backed up by practical experiences are the most likely retained by the learners. They are easy to recall because they are both associated with the sense of sight, taste, sound, feeling, or smell and are interpreted somewhat differently by the mind. Students gain a better understanding, a broader view of the world, an appreciation of community, insight into their skills, interests, passions, and values, opportunities to collaborate, positive professional practices, and self-confidence. Thus, experience has been described as the best teacher.

The totality, therefore, of one's everyday life sums up as his experience - whether dull or brilliant, negative or positive. Interestingly, the quality of life an individual possesses is tied to their experiences and how they allow these encounters to shape their decision-making and positioning for the future they want. Hence, there is a need for intentionality.

The intentionality required entails assembling previous learning experiences to produce a new pattern of behaviour. This is known as reasoning. It pays off when one can relive past experiences, reflect on them, and discover new insights. Therefore, the quality of reasoning is enhanced by the type and depth of experiences, as reasoning cannot go outside the perimeters of experience. The richer the experience, the better one can apply oneself to high-level reasoning. The overall interplay of experiences and reasoning can assist with contextualising one's current contexts and ongoing learning and navigating future experiences for new lessons and continuous growth.

As we did at LiME, people are exposed to new paradigms and viewpoints through tasks, projects, fun stuffs, training, mentorship, and coaching. As a result of the experience, they can engage their senses, improve their cognition, and engage in high-level reasoning. They ask questions of themselves and others in the relevant groups and sphere of influence, question assumptions, explore alternative solutions, and try out new things to better themselves and others. They engaged the power of critical thinking and problem-solving.

Experience, Critical Thinking, and Problem Solving

Critical thinking involves the active conceptualisation, synthesis, and application of the information gathered from observations, reflections, and communication. Together, these become a guide to belief and action towards engaging the future.

This remarkable skill is developed through practice and experience. It enables one to appreciate that there are always options, even when making decisions and solving problems. Furthermore, it allows one to compare the pros and cons of the available options and make informed decisions in the context of conflicting priorities.

Problem-solving skills have become very relevant and highly-sought soft skills in recent times. It requires one to apply intelligence and an out-of-the-box approach to proffering solutions to problems. This becomes even more relevant when faced with unforeseen issues that are often ambiguous and multilayered. The onus is then on the individual to critically analyse the nature of the problem, find a fitting solution for it, and take necessary actions to implement the solution.

In the context of experience, other relevant skills are closely related to reasoning, critical thinking, and problem-solving skills. Solving the real-world problems and challenges of the 21st century also involves creative, collaborative, and communication skills. LiMERs have largely attributed their acquisition of these skills to their LiME experience.

LiME Exposure and Dynamism

LiME was designed and delivered in the spirit that real learning goes beyond the traditional education system. We prefaced it on the principle that one should not only connect school activities and students' everyday life experiences but the two should leverage each other positively. LiME provided opportunities for direct and positive interaction - social, mental, and physical.

LiME demonstrates that youth from diverse cultural backgrounds have a lot to offer to countries and communities that validate their relevance and give them the opportunity and enabling environment to lead and flourish.

LiME exposed participants to a diversity of experiences:

- Learning and gathering relevant knowledge and skills via the seminars, one-to-one, and group training sessions, etc.,

- Travelling to places and experiencing the dynamics of our contemporary world,

- Interacting with new people and cultures,

- Participating in local and international events (LiMErs were invited as valued speakers and presenters in some),

- Acquiring emotional and cultural intelligence, which are so relevant for our times,

- Navigating the maze and complexities of collaborations and relationships, and

- Taking on challenging tasks and projects with significant impacts and benefits.

Experiences Through LiME Projects

Let's relive a few of the LiME projects that provided participants with some of these experiences, just presenting the highlights.

Excursion to BHP

The LiME facilitated and well-managed excursion to one of Australia's biggest multinational companies and mining giant, BHP, is an example of the types of exposure and experiences provided to the youth and young people in the program. LiME youth had a dedicated tour of BHP's state-of-the-art Integrated Remote Operations Centre (IROC). They also mingled with professionals at the centre.

There was intentionality in making room for time, space, and engagement to ask questions and receive first-hand information and answers about the technological advancement in the IROC. It also involved open conversations about career prospects in BHP and the resource industry. Then, of course, there was lunch. LiMErs and their peers have never stopped talking about the benefits of that experiential tour. What a lasting impact!

LiME Book Project

The LiME book project involved leadership and teamwork in action. It incorporated envisioning, goal-setting, project management, critical thinking, and problem-solving skills. LiMErs brainstormed various options of challenges to take on together. They finally chose to author a book highlighting their experiences in the context of contemporary issues they confront daily. Yes, they were supported by mentors and experienced writers, but they did it.

Professionally and successfully, they undertook the project, including working to a defined scope, associating tasks, assigning resources, and setting the budget and timeline for completing the work. They researched the relevant topics, brainstormed them further, and wrote the chapters as assigned. It was a remarkable achievement for LiMErs when they launched their book *"A Handbook for Migrant Youth: Peer to Peer Wisdom from Those Who've Been There, Done That"* in 2019.

LiME Podcast Series

LiMErs undertook another leadership-by-doing project during 2020 / 2021, where they led a 7-part live podcast series on relevant topics, including multiculturalism, education, employment, technology, social media, mental health, and finance. The topics were aligned with those in their book. It was, indeed, a build-up on the experience of the authorship of their book. The former gained from the momentum in achieving the latter.

They engaged with the community, especially youth and young people like them. They shared knowledge, inspiration, and experiences. They took the risk of doing the series live to ensure they preserved the authenticity and courage in embarking on such a project. Their response to what is considered a reasonable suggestion, i.e., to pre-record the conversations and show clips for the podcast series: "No, let's do it live. If we make mistakes, so be it; we will apologise to our audience, adjust, and get on with the live podcasts."

They did it. It turned out that there were minimal and almost unrecognisable errors throughout the series. This was another avenue in which they demonstrated that 'failing fast, failing small, and failing forward' worked well. Indeed, LiME is a proven model for unleashing greatness. LiMErs are still receiving feedback on the impact of the series – economically, socially, and globally.

These valuable experiences have shown that learning goes beyond the academic frontiers of the traditional educational system and transcends into everyday living. Moreover, they have contributed to building and nurturing individuals into astute leaders as they continue to unleash the greatness in them. Anecdotes from some former LiME participants are presented in the next section.

Some LiME Testimonials

King David was the LiME youth peer leader. He heartily affirms the unique benefits of LiME exposure and continues to use the acquired skills in his ongoing leading roles in his community and work. He has been a keynote speaker at major events and conferences. King David has since completed his study and secured gainful employment in the health and retail industry.

Keyshiaa attributes her renewed confidence to the LiME experience she has had. She has secured a few volunteering and paid roles in the professional services and early childhood industry. She never stops talking about how much she has been practising her exposure to the great principle that stuck with her: *'Fail Fast', 'Fail Small, and 'Fail Forward'*. Keyshiaa is a passionate crusader of the positive LiME impact.

Niche has been a keynote speaker at the highly regarded City of Gosnell's event with guests including members of parliament, mayors, council members, etc. He was also an invited speaker at an international event, Lead India. Again, he shined through that as well. The confidence and intelligence with which he speaks continue to open up more opportunities for him. He was selected as part of Western Australia's inaugural student council 2022. Niche wrote to Ephraim (LiME founder) on receiving the great news:

> *"I just want to thank you for the opportunities that LiME has given me. It has been a life-changing experience being part of this journey, and also, thank you so much for putting my leadership into motion and experience!"*

Maria displayed so much confidence and professionalism while giving a keynote speech at a conference. The positive feedback from the organisers and attendees of that conference further indicates how the LiME initiative has positively impacted youth and young folks. Maria has since gained admission into one of the universities in Western Australia to study Pharmacy. She is also the resident designer for a custom cake specialist organisation. She has the potential and capacity to continue to unleash greatness in her life and her world.

LiME founder and other key players cannot guarantee that every LiMEr will continue to unleash their greatness. Indeed, it experienced its fair share of challenges – during design, planning, and implementation. However, these testimonials indicate that the seed has been sown with evidence of germination and appreciable levels of growth and impact. Maybe more realistically, it can be reignited, replicated, and extended.

CHAPTER 6
LiME TRIALS AND TRIUMPHS

"When things do not go your way, remember that every challenge – every adversity – contains within it the seeds of opportunity and growth."

Roy T. Benett

The LiME journey to date has not been smooth all the way. There were a few bumps and turbulences. Nevertheless, like everything valuable, the pain and perseverance in steadying the vehicle through the process were worth it. The LiME coordinating team adopted the wisdom of what Max DePree, an American businessman and writer, once said, *"The first responsibility of a leader is to define reality. The last is to say thank you. In between, the leader is a servant."* The team did not underestimate the reality of the situation on the ground.

However, beyond the challenges, the team envisioned the greatness ahead through the lenses of possibilities, purpose, and passion and served accordingly. We took every challenge as a stepping stone along the path of progress. We kept practising what we were teaching LiME youth – *failing fast, failing small, and failing forward.* We were agile in our approach, including starting imperfectly in many instances, celebrating small wins, embracing change, learning and adjusting quickly as necessary, and ensuring delivery of value for LiMErs and the broader community along the way. Next, we present a few of these trials and how we triumphed.

Recruiting Participating Youth

Invitations and expressions of interest were sent to several young people to participate in LiME. Unfortunately, a significant proportion did not respond. Some of them declined outrightly. The feedback indicated that they faced hurdles related to personal issues, peer influence, difficult family situations, etc. Some were held back by thinking, "*I am not enough for this leadership thing.*" Others were negatively influenced by suggestions that "*such programs are a waste of time.*" Some prospective LiMErs lacked the logistic and moral support typically provided within the family context.

The feedback to our invitations also implied some form of the nonchalant attitude of some youth towards leadership development. This was a bit alarming, considering the fierceness of the odds against the younger generation in contemporary times. How would they overcome the onslaught of mixed messages and often negative social media influences? How would they develop the self-awareness, self-worth, and confidence (like what LiME teaches) to make wise decisions that will work for them despite the often conflicting messages and influences from peers?

Thankfully, some families can provide the foundations and safety nets required to give an excellent start for the young people in such families. What about those that may not be as lucky? Would they not need to participate in programs like LiME to help fill the gaps? These hurdles did limit the opportunities for more youth to join LiME despite their potential and aspirations to pursue excellence in leadership. The passion for positive change drove LiME coordinators into problem-solving mode, and we found some solutions.

Firstly, we started from our own families. *Charity begins at home*. After all, our children also require the self-development and leadership skills that LiME offers. Then, we campaigned vigorously in the schools and communities where LiME coordinators and our children are already known, including a network of friends, neighbours, and colleagues. Finally, LiME coordinators went the extra mile in arranging additional logistics, including car-pooling, which were doable to ensure that serious-minded prospective LiMErs did not miss out.

LiMErs from fourteen diverse national and cultural backgrounds were signed up for the inaugural LiME phase in 2018. That number and diversity grew with subsequent phases. More importantly, we remain thankful to LiME youth and their parents/guardians for the trust and belief.

Finding Coordinators, Mentors, and Facilitators

People are generally time-poor these days. There are numerous and often essential tasks to fill in the days. Moreover, we prioritise our endeavours so that activities and projects that matter more would receive more commitment from our limited time and scarce resources. Thus, the question was, how much would LiME matter? What's the ranking in the context of all other endeavours? The founder may not have this challenge since commencing LiME was already a burden he had to attend to, one way or the other. But he cannot implement the vision alone. The challenge was how he could sell the idea to others working with him to deliver LiME. He did just that.

LiME founder was already leading a team and network of collaborators in Multicultural Professional Bridge (MPB), which is like the same genre as LiME, but this time with adult participation. The cohort of people already connected to MPB at various levels – board membership, volunteers, and participants – agreed with the LiME founder that both share similar concerns and solutions.

Thus, the pioneering coordinators, mentors, and facilitators were mainly a shared resource structure between both initiatives. As required, we only needed to fill the gaps with other fresh resources.

The business model for LiME delivery was primarily humanitarian and not profit-driven. This has its challenges. The coordinators, mentors, and facilitators were volunteers, even though most could have charged top-dollar for similar work in their regular professional spaces. On the flip side, the LiME founder/leader had to work out the flexibility required in LiME delivery to ensure that the demand for volunteers' time and logistics did not exceed expectations. Indeed, they were so selfless that they went over and above their commitments in sowing time and resources to equipping and empowering LiME youth. For this, we remain thankful.

Funding the Vision

Resources – people, tools, funds, etc., fuel vision. But quite often, they are limited. Like the American-Indian Author and Entrepreneur, C.K Prahalad said, *"limited resources are stretched to fit ambitious aspirations."* Unfortunately, such limitations have caused the abortion of many promising and socially impactful ventures.

As reported in the last section, finding and retaining committed volunteers was a challenging part of this LiME initiative, like many others. Thankfully, LiME was blessed with a handful of people with great minds that contributed at various levels as coordinators, mentors, and facilitators. More often, though, one would have to pay for some roles. Offering discounted rates is usually the available concession in such situations, which was the case with the LiME initiative.

In addition to paying for people's time and unavoidable services, funding is also required for renting venues (for training, seminars, mentorship sessions, fun times, etc.), tools like audiovisual systems, and other items like stationary, subscriptions, etc. But, again, the LiME coordinating team went into problem-solving and was able to secure a couple of grants from local and state governments, which did help to meet these commitments reasonably well.

While we set a boundary of what could be done, due to these limitations of participants and resources, we did enough to deliver three phases of LiME to date successfully. Despite the various challenges and trials experienced, the team kept a steady focus on the vision of unleashing greatness in youth. As a result, we triumphed because we served in the spirit of possibilities, purpose, and passion.

CHAPTER 7
CONCLUSION

Thank you for journeying with me to the final words in this book. I am excited about the exposure and enlightenment you've grasped from the pages of this book. I want to see more people unleash their greatness in them with a sense of passion and purpose. Whenever we consider the hands that lift glistening trophies, the heads that wear jewelled crowns, and the necks adorned with Olympic gold medals, one thing is sure: they chose to unleash the greatness within. They put in the hard work. They took ownership of their lives and their destinies. They were leaders of their futures.

The LiME leadership model is designed and implemented on the critical principles of mastering the inner game and leading inside-out. It involves discovering self and valuing one's identity. Then, we develop this valued self without necessarily giving in to the unrelenting pressure of comparison with the *other celebrated and less-authentic images*. It is also vital to be agile while maintaining the core balance of self. This includes putting oneself out there, keeping up with technology, being physically active, and maintaining the child-like fun of life. A LiME leader is open to diverse experiences while building the core of his or her uniqueness.

LiME has helped talented youth win the battles against identity issues, conflicting priorities, low self-worth, lack of motivation, and underperformance, often preventing people from becoming their best versions. Knowing who you are is paramount to your commitment and drive. Until you come to a point where you understand your place and purpose in the tide of life, you'll continue to struggle with reality. Imagine square pegs trying to fit in round holes.

CONCLUSION

The heartbeat of LiME is teaching, inspiring, connecting, and challenging youth of diverse cultural backgrounds to discover themselves, silence every clanging cymbal of doubt and resounding bells of defeat that resonates within their minds, and help them release their potentials and greatness.

The LiME model has been successfully tested with youth. It will work for people of all ages as long as they are ready to work the winning principles that unleash greatness.

LiME: LEADERSHIP in MOTION & EXPERIENCE

*LiME is **global***

Maiden LiME Youth Participants: they are already influencing their world[13]

---

[13] A Handbook for Migrant Youth: Peer To Peer Wisdom From Those Who've Been There, Done That (2019: back-cover page).

LiMErs and the LiME model are catalysts for unleashing greatness across generations and geographical locations.

Started down-under in Australia; growing across the globe.

You may be interested in this book
by **LiME Youth**

A HANDBOOK *for* MIGRANT YOUTH

PEER TO PEER WISDOM FROM THOSE WHO'VE BEEN THERE, DONE THAT

LiME Youth
Compiled by Ephraim Osaghae

A Handbook for Migrant Youth

Peer To Peer Wisdom From Those Who've Been There, Done That

A Glimpse into the World of Migrant Youth. A vibrant group of multicultural youth group presents what it takes to make it as a young migrant - to live to the fullest, to achieve your dreams and to enjoy the experience. Prepare yourself for insights, stories and lessons from their lives, and the acumen they have gathered from the *LiME Project*.

All young people, migrants as well as those who are already established in the new country will find information in this book very useful. And they can use it to inspire others as well.

Parents, mentors, teachers, and school administrators will find valuable tips and suggestions in this book that will help them in their ongoing efforts to make great leaders of their children, mentees, and students.

The content in this book will also provide government office holders, policymakers and service providers with real stories and lived experiences from young people.

Finally, while Australia is the context for this book, the principles and lessons are applicable across the globe.

You may also be interested in the following books by **Ephraim Osaghae**

A Handbook for Migrants: The Good, The Challenges and The Lessons

A Reflective Guide for Meaningful and Whole-Life Experience

In this book, you will find the following:

- Who really is a migrant?
- The career and business challenges of a migrant; and proposed solutions.
- The challenges and lessons with regards to family life including raising children and youths.
- The essential aspects and preparation for aging and retirement.
- The importance of communities and leadership.
- The lived experiences of a migrant.

You will find great use for the content of this book if you are:

- Intending migrants looking for pre-migration considerations and tips.
- Migrants looking for guidance in work, families, youths, and community engagements.
- Non-migrants, students, policymakers, service providers and community leaders.

This book also allows you to participate in meaningful conversations on migrant experiences.

Adopt Adapt Achieve

An Amazing Triple A Guide for Successful Relocation, Change and Integration

Written for all ages and cultural backgrounds, this extraordinary story takes about an hour to read, but the insights can last a lifetime, with knowledge you can hand down to future generations.

This book reveals hard and unknown truths about relocation, change and integration. And focuses on crucial tactics to **Adopt** and **Adapt** to **Achieve** your goals for the big move.

The author of the book writes from two decades of personal experiences and research in relocating from Africa to Australia - the many successes to enjoy, the pitfalls to avoid, and principles for guidance. The narrative includes snippets from his in-depth interactions with diverse members of the community including immigrants, students, professionals, locals, service providers, workers, business people, government officials, and policymakers.

When you know the real stories of real people, you can prepare yourself better on how to deal with change. You can be careful not to repeat mistakes and go on with less stress and more success in your journey even as you consider your family, career, and healthy ageing.

Non-immigrants will find useful hints and tips in reading this book given the increasing need for cultural integration in our schools, workplaces, neighbourhoods, and communities.

Voices from Home: Wisdom from Our Diasporic Roots

A Narration of Parents of First-Generation Migrants

Every human being is part of a bigger family, which is figuratively represented by the family tree. We have roots that extend beyond places and cultures of our current residences. Our roots still weigh a lot into our everyday living irrespective of geographical distance and time.

- This book will provide inspiration, some incentives, and a compass for teachable minds to explore and tap into the wealth of their roots.

- It provides insights on the key dynamics and interplay of cultures, underpinning motivations, and extended family structures of typical first-generation migrants.

- It informs global audiences about lived experiences of people of migrant backgrounds starting with the Australian context.

- It contributes to the value-adding conversations around the themes of identity, cross-cultural intelligence, sustainable migration, etc.

- It provides hints and tips for relevant policy makers, service providers, and other government officials, especially in the areas of sustainable migration.

HOW TO ACHIEVE SUCCESSFUL MIGRATION AND INTEGRATION

Turning what could have been threats and weaknesses to opportunities and strengths

WORKBOOK

EPHRAIM OSAGHAE MBL, PMP, MBA

How to Achieve Successful Migration and Integration (Workbook)

Turning what could have been threats and weaknesses to opportunities and strengths

The focus of this workbook is to provide practical information and wisdom for getting the best value out of the investments in the big move of migration, relocation, and integration.

The key aspects of migration value chain are covered in the book including factors to consider as part of pre-migration preparations, setting SMART goals, and settling well into your new location.

Learn:

- How to prepare prior to your relocation
- How to transition and settle well in the new location
- How to adopt, adapt and be successful in achieving your goals
- How to sustain the achievement of your goals

Readers and users will learn and receive guidance based on real stories of real people that should lead to real actions for success.

Top Insiders Guide To Successful And Stable Careers

How to Secure and Sustain Professional Jobs Without Losing Self and Value

From two decades of lived experiences (as a skilled immigrant himself, residential professional, and expat work in Africa, Australia, The Middle East, Europe, USA, and Asia, and his extensive NGO work), Ephraim Osaghae addresses tough questions about navigating your new country for successful and stable careers.

He believes that when you learn from real stories of real people and selfless insiders, you can prepare yourself better on how to deal with change, relocation, and other major shifts in life. You can take the necessary actions to maximize gains, minimize pains, and achieve your goals.

This quick and easy-to-read guide book:

- Unpacks the foundational principles of maximizing your strengths, managing your weaknesses, and achieving your goals.

- Reveals master frameworks for communication, qualifications, work experience, and networking.

- Teaches you to understand the critical place of showing up!

While intending, new and relatively more settled immigrants are the ideal audience for this book, non-immigrants and other stakeholders will also find useful hints and tips for job-seeking and cultural intelligence.

Migrapreneurs

The Potentials for Diversifying our Diversity

Immigrants are people who have moved to new countries in order to settle as permanent residents or naturalized citizens. This valuable resource is primarily for them; especially those having doubts about their potentials and entrepreneurial skills, and applying the advantages in their new locations.

Give a man (or a woman) a fish and you feed him for a day;
Teach a man (or a woman) to fish and you feed him for a lifetime;
What about the man or woman owning a pond or two containing fishes?

This book provides exclusive insights into Migrapreneurs (migrants + entrepreneurship), the who, what, why, and how. It will inform, inspire, and challenge readers to courageously exploit the advantages of their diversity in the context of entrepreneurship and business. They can take charge of their destinies by creating robust options while depending less on the already challenged economic and social welfare systems in the new countries.

Before you start reading, please prepare your mind for a journey that requires discipline and focus. What this book offers you is a path most immigrants don't take due to can't-do mindset, scarcity mentality, fear of the unknown, and lack of appropriate support. Reading this book, and taking prescribed actions, will assuredly provide you with a trigger for getting on the path to greatness.

Migration And Family

Secrets to Sustainability for Culturally Diverse Families

Family in the context of migration and cultural diversity is rarely discussed at the gates of ideas today. Search Amazon or Google, and you'll be amazed at how well we've avoided this subject. Yet, a happy home is critical to life abroad or anywhere for that matter.

Resident in Australia, Ephraim Osaghae, has taken the lid off several hot migration topics in his books. *MIGRATION AND FAMILY* is one of his best works.

Few matters in life go deep, wide, and have a lasting impact like family. Ignoring what happens to the family unit means treating symptoms without removing the source of illness or cutting the branches without touching the roots.

Drawing from the depth of researched insights and lived experiences, Ephraim:

- -Reveals critical links between immigration and multicultural families.
- -Offers thriving tools and tips for fixing migrant and culturally diverse family issues.
- -Advocates better family-friendly immigration policies.
- -Provides some future projections.

Ephraim is not shifting blames. He's providing timely wisdom for multicultural individuals, families, and communities, as well as colleagues, neighbours, service providers, and other stakeholders. Pick this book and get one for someone. You'll look back and thank yourself.

www.ingramcontent.com/pod-product-compliance
Lightning Source LLC
Chambersburg PA
CBHW070309010526
44107CB00056B/2545